He's Coming *Like A* Thief

DIANE HASTINGS

WESTBOW
PRESS®
A DIVISION OF THOMAS NELSON
& ZONDERVAN

WestBow Press books may be ordered through
booksellers or by contacting:

WestBow Press
A Division of Thomas Nelson & Zondervan
1663 Liberty Drive
Bloomington, IN 47403
www.westbowpress.com
844-714-3454

All Scripture quotations are taken from the King James Version.

ISBN: 978-1-6642-3399-7 (sc)
ISBN: 978-1-6642-3400-0 (e)

Library of Congress Control Number: 2021909610

Print information available on the last page.

WestBow Press rev. date: 5/17/2021

CONTENTS

Contents

INTRODUCTION

THE BOOK HE'S COMING like a thief is to inform, enlighten, and bring awareness about the soon coming King. The warning signs are out there. Will you be ready? God's word tells us that he wants no one to perish but that we should repent. He has a better place for us in heaven and (Jesus) went to prepare that place for us. Time is winding up. In this book you will find scriptures to verify or prove that God's Son is returning soon. But there are also other scriptures to show you how to position yourself and be ready for his return. The first one is Romans 10:9 & 13, the next one is Isaiah 55:6, 2 Timothy 2:15, Ephesians 6:10 -18 and many other scriptures to help you to stand. You will have to pray without ceasing. Meditate and study the word of God because you want to be rooted and grounded in the Lord. That is the only way that you will be able to make it. This book talks about the craftiness of the thief and how quickly he comes and goes. That is how quick the Lord is coming. When he comes it will be like a thief in the night, when no one was expecting him to come. No one was watching or they were not paying attention. Watch and pray that ye do not enter into temptation. I hope this book encourage you and also strengthen you as well. Knowing that God is soon to return, and also letting you know to get ready and prepare yourself.

ACKNOWLEDGEMENTS

I THANK GOD FOR allowing me to be a messenger of his word by mouth, singing, and by pen and paper. I love the pen and paper part because when you write, it is basically you and God. You will not have anyone disagreeing or giving their opinion about what God has given you to say. And when you write, your words can go all over the world and reach the masses. Books and the written word can go into places where you may never go. I dedicate this book to my late spouse whom I lost suddenly from the corona virus and that is a part of what inspired this book. " He's Coming Like A Thief". He as well as other's have lost their lives through this wicked and fierce virus. He was gone in less then a month from being diagnosed. It went very quickly. And I believe that is why God said to write this book to let others know. I also dedicate this book to my Mom and other family members who has passed on. I thank God for my fellow comrades in the Gospel for their prayers and support during this writing process and holding me up in prayer. But most of all I thank Jesus for mercy and grace. I thank him for giving his life for me. I thank God for giving us his Son.

Chapter One

THE THIEF

∞

THIS CHAPTER DESCRIBES THE actions of a thief. The thief is one who catches you off guard or when you are not expecting him to come. He is sly and he is sneaky. He is studying your everyday routine. And he does all of this while planning his next move. He knows what time you leave and what time you arrive back home. He knows if you are alone or if you have someone living in the house with you. He also knows if you have a pet living with you or if you have an alarm system because he is studying you. He is skillful and plots every step that you make. He plans how he is going to enter and which way he is going to exit the house. The thief is someone that comes in when you least expect him to, and he comes to rob or steal from you. Most of the time he comes at night when you are asleep or he may come when you are away from the house. Either way he slips in and out so quickly that you are not even aware that he has been there until you start noticing some things missing or out of place. Sometimes the thief will even tear up or destroy your house or things in your house, like pictures, furniture, walls, and things of that nature. When I looked at the meaning of a thief it said the thief" is one who steals the goods and property of another" he did not buy it and it was not given to him by the owner. That is why it is particularly important to watch your surroundings. Because a thief comes when you are not looking. You are so caught up with life that you do not recognize that you are being watched. And that is talking about the physical or natural thief. This book is talking about the spiritual thief which is describing how Jesus' second coming is going to be. People are going to be going about their everyday business, working, marrying, having children, and everything else that comes with life and trying to make it. That they are not even aware that the Lord is on his way back to get his own. They are not watching the signs according to Matthews in the Bible when it tells us about all the things that are going to happen. We have to watch and pray because it also tells us if we endure unto the end we will be saved. Trials and test will come but be encourage. Don't give up.Hold on and do not quit. We are living in perilous

times. Families are revolting against each other. Some
of them have no morals, no values, they are very selfish,
weak, disrespectful, lovers of pleasure more than lovers
of God. God's word is being fulfilled every day. Repent
and turn from your wicked ways. God is coming back
sooner than we think. He is coming with a vengeance
and for a church without spot or wrinkle. No one will
be able to escape his wrath. God is an all seeing and
all-knowing God. He knows what is going on with
you. Vine's Expository Dictionary of Old and New
Testament words describes a thief as this (c) figuratively,
(I) of the personal coming of Christ, in a warning to a
local church, with most of its members possessed of
mere outward profession and defiled by the world.`"'
Revelation 3:3; in retributive intervention to overthrow
the foes of God, Revelation 16:15; and "(2)" of the Day of
the Lord, in divine judgment upon the world," "2 Peter
3:10 and 1 Thessalonians 5: 2 & 4". God is warning
us about the thief, but he is also reminding us that we
as saints of God are not in darkness therefore that day
will not overtake us. His word tells us not to sleep, as
do others but watch and be sober, be alert, be wise
to the signs of the coming of the Lord. It is coming
quick, and it is coming swift as in a twinkling of the
eyes. Now blink your eyes for me. Do you see how
fast that was? His word says it and that settles it in the
heavens. Proverbs 4:7 says, "Wisdom is the principal

thing; therefore get wisdom: and with all thy getting get understanding." Understand this the prophecy is real. God is on his way back to open the heavens. It is no time to play or guess. You may say it is not real or he is not coming. I say if you don't believe this is real,then what is it to live a clean, free, and holy life? Now look at it this way. What if this is real and it is? And you did not take the opportunity to get in right standing with the Lord? You just lost your life and soul over opinions and unbelief. Is it worth all of that? Don't play rushing roulette with your life.

Chapter Two

NIGHT TIME

∞

IN THIS CHAPTER I will discuss the night time. Night time is darkness where no one can see without candles or light. Nighttime is sometimes dreary and dark. You sometimes feel dread or heaviness. We are talking about the night because the name of this book is "He's coming like a thief". The reference scripture for this book comes from 1 Thessalonians 5:2 "For yourselves know perfectly that the day of the Lord so cometh as a thief in the night". Meaning unawares, suddenly without warning. When it is night or pitch black you cannot see what is in front of you. So, if you cannot see what is in front of you naturally or spiritually, that means you are not watching or praying, and you will not know when Jesus comes because you are spiritually asleep. The Webster's Revised Unabridged Dictionary according to google search says it like this for night" 2. (n) Darkness; Obscurity; Concealment. 3. (n) Intellectual and moral darkness; not knowing or ignoring what's morally right. Or we choose not to do what is right". Some of us are spiritually blind and cannot see because we are walking in the carnal mind and not the spiritual mind. And that is a sign of being in spiritual darkness or being in the night. When you are spiritually blind you stumble in the dark and cannot see your way through. Vine's Expository Dictionary says night like this" of the period of absence of light, the time in which something takes place, e.g.," most of the time that is when the thief comes. When no one can see him, or you are asleep. That is when you are at your most vulnerable state because your guard is down. The New Webster's Dictionary & Roget's Thesaurus describes their night as this" the time of darkness from sunset to sunrise; end of day light; intellectual or spiritual darkness; ignorance; death." intellectual darkness is not having the power to understand or not having intellect. When you do not understand the principles of God or his word you will not be able to discern the signs about the coming of the Lord. This is because you are unable to understand the word of God. Ignorance is just being uninformed or unlearned. You cannot be informed or learn anything pertaining to the word of God unless you have an instructor to help you, or you study the word of God for yourself and pray and ask God to reveal to you what he wants you to know out of it. When God opens his word to you then you can understand and know about his promises and your future in him. Also, you will see scriptures telling you about certain signs in his word. Although no one knows when he is coming back. You will at least know that it is near because of the prophecies and seeing certain events already taking place. According to "ChristianAnswer.Net" Spiritual Darkness is a symptom of spiritual death". St. John 11:10 says" But if a man walk in the night, he stumbleth, because there is no light in him". These different types of nights show us how we can be in the dark and miss the coming of our Lord and savior. So, open up your spiritual eyes and be on the lookout. He's coming sooner than you think.

Chapter Three

THE PURPOSE OF HIS COMING

∞

THE PURPOSE OF CHRIST'S coming is to receive you and I unto himself. When he left here, he said that he was going away to prepare a place for us so we can be where he is. When he comes back, he will be fulfilling the Gospel and his promise. Christ is faithful to all of his promises. He has not let any of his words fall to the ground. He cannot lie. He is coming back to gather his elect. Matthew 24:31 tells us" And he shall send his angels with a great sound of a trumpet, and they shall gather together his elect from the four winds, from one end of heaven to the other". He is coming back to raise the dead in Christ. 1 Thessalonians 4:16 says "for the Lord himself shall descend from heaven with a shout, with the voice of the archangel, and with the trump of God: and the dead in Christ shall rise first:" He is coming to destroy death. 1 Corinthians 15:25 & 26 says 25" For he must reign, till he hath put all enemies under his feet". 26" The last enemy that shall be destroyed is death". He is coming to judge the world. Matthew 25: 32-46 verses. He is coming to glorify the believers. Colossians 3:4 says" When Christ, who is our life, shall appear, then shall ye also appear with him in glory". He is coming to reward the people of God. Matthew 16:27 tells us "for the Son of man shall come in the glory of his Father with his angels; and then he shall reward every man according to his works". Christ is coming without warning anyone,and he is coming with a fire. In the Old and New Testament scriptures it tells us about God's judgment and how he used fire to punish those that were wicked, disobedient or sinning. The book of Revelation really stands out when it talks about God's justice and the final scene. It talks about the devil that deceived God's people and what his future was going to be and how he was going to be thrown into a lake of fire and brim stones. It talked about how the angel of God poured out a vial upon the sun and he was given power to scorch men with fire. God's wrath is going to be fierce. Everyone will have to stand before the judgment seat. No one shall escape this final step. Revelation 20:14 & 15 says 14" And death and hell were cast into the lake of fire. This is the second death". 15"

And whosoever was not found written in the book of life was cast into the lake of fire". These scriptures and quotes are explaining the purpose of his coming and what the end will be. And now since you know what to expect and that he is coming with a purpose it is time that you prepare yourselves.

Chapter Four

THE COMING OF
THE LORD

∞

IN THE NEW TESTAMENT Christ talks about his coming. When he comes this second time, he is coming to judge the world. If you read in Revelation, it talks about a series of events that will take place when the tribulation period starts. The coming of the Lord is going to be a day of rejoicing and a day of trouble. It will be joy for the elect and trouble for the sinners. For the ones that will be alive you will see the son of man coming with the angels and in God's glory. The Lord is going to repay each and everyone for the deeds that he has done. Whether good or bad. Some people want even taste death until you see him come. When I looked up the word come it says coming means" approaching; arriving; arriving at some state or condition; moving towards; reaching; happening (to); originating; occurring; appearing; turning out to be. And really this comes from the root word of (come). So, if we look at some of these words you will see approaching, drawing near or coming near. This let's us know that the time of Christ's coming is really soon. Romans 13:11-14 tells us what we should be doing. It tells us that since we know the hour is near and that it is high time, we should be awake and not sleep. That our salvation is closer then when we first believed and accepted the Lord. Our night is far spent, and the day is almost here. Therefore, we need to cast off every work of darkness, and put on the armor of light. This mean it is time to turn the things that are not pleasing to God around and walk in the light of God and not in darkness. We must walk honestly, not in riotous living or drunkenness, not living in strife or envying one another. But putting on the Lord Jesus and not making provision for our flesh. We are trying to fulfill worldly lust and fleshly lust or trying to satisfy our flesh. The bible tells us to walk in the spirit and not fulfill the lust of the flesh. Our flesh does not want to suffer. It wants to be comfortable and have pleasure in things. Some of us have a big problem with the lust of the eyes. This can get us into trouble and caught up into things that you do not want to be in. Or it can take you places that you do not want to go if you are not careful. The bible tells us that we are not ignorant of Satan devices. He is cunning and crafty. That is why you must be ready and recognize his tactics. So, you will not miss the coming of the Lord. In Revelation Christ tells us that he is coming quickly; and that he has a reward with him, to give each and every man according to the work that he has done. Revelation 22:7 says "Behold, I come quickly: blessed is he that keepeth the sayings of the prophecy of this book". In the book of Revelation John is saying that these sayings are true and faithful: and that the Lord of the holy prophets sent angels to show John the things that shall shortly be done. The Lord is coming. Be prepared, watchful, and diligent about his coming and the work of God.

Chapter Five

NO ONE KNOWS
THE TIME

∞

NO ONE KNOWS THE time that the Lord will come.
I believe scholars, theologians, scientist, and others are
still trying to figure out when this great and terrible
day of the Lord is. They search the scriptures in the
bible to see all the signs and if everything that was said
is happening or if some of these things have already
happen. The same way it was in the days of Noah when
men and women were drinking and getting married is
going to be the same way it is going to be even now.
That is why it tells us in the bible to watch and pray
because we do not know when all these things are
going take place. You do not want to be left behind or
be put into eternal damnation for not being ready. If
the Son of man and the angels were not aware of that

day, you know we will not know of Christ's return either. Only our Father in heaven knows about the day of the Lord. The bible tells us to take heed because we do not know the actual time and that we should be very alert. I am saying to you do not sleep or slumber because time is winding up for us all. Ephesians 5:15,16 & 17 says "15. See then that ye walk circumspectly, not as fools, but as wise,"16. Redeeming the time, because the days are evil"." 17. Wherefore be ye not unwise, but understanding what the will of the Lord is". This is telling us to take heed and not be foolish. We are living in a wicked and evil world. People are very cruel and hateful. So, this means we need to use wisdom in our daily walk with God. Making sure we are saved and ministering the gospel of Jesus Christ. We need to understand our purpose and what the will of God is for our lives and start operating in it. We do not have to be slipping and sliding or putting ourselves in compromising situations.We can live right. Christ was our example. If he made it we can. Here in Matthew 24:36 Jesus explains "But of that day and hour knoweth no man, no, not the angels of heaven, but my father only". We have scriptures telling us that only God knows of the day and time that his Son will return. You know how when the news casters forecast rain, snow, tornado's, hurricanes', etc. we start preparing and planning emergency exits routes, and getting emergency foods, flashlights, water, blankets, candles, and a place we can go for shelter and safety. This is what we need to do as well. Plan for our holy emergency exits. We do not look at it that way but that is what we need to do. We need to get us a holy bunker where we can lay before God and begin to seek him like we have never done before. We need to get our bibles, bless oil, pen, and paper and put it in our emergency care package. We need our prayer shawls to wrap up in and let God's anointing flow through us as we pray and seek God. This is us spiritually preparing for the coming of the Lord. Matthew 24:44 tells us." Therefore be ye also ready: for in such an hour as ye think not the Son of man cometh". There it is again when we are not thinking about him then he appears. The bible tells us he that has ears to hear then let him hear what the church is sayings. Well, the church saying repent for the kingdom of God is at hand. The church is saying that God so loved us that he gave Jesus for our sins and for salvation. The church is saying it is holiness or hell. The church is saying get your life right people and let us go home. In other words, let us get it together so we will be ready to go back with the Lord when he comes. The church is saying I am here if you need prayer or someone to talk to. The church is saying let us walk this walk out together. Let us not leave anyone behind. John 1:12 says" But as many as received him, to them gave he power to become the sons of God, even to them that believe on his name:" The way has been made people all we have to do is believe on his name, receive him, and live right.

Chapter Six

BE PREPARED

∞

TO BE PREPARED MEANS you must be ready at all times. No matter what you must face. When you are prepared you can tackle any problem or situation. One way to prepare yourself is by putting on the whole armor of God. Ephesians 6:10-18 will explain some of the different parts of the armor that is important to wear. In the Webster's dictionary it describes the word prepare as this" make ready for use; to fit for a particular purpose; to make oneself ready. And the New Unger's Bible dictionary said it like this for preparation" (a making ready) "In the Vine's Expository dictionary it says for the words (preparation, prepare, prepared) and it denotes (a) readiness, (b) preparation; it is found in Ephesians. 6: 15 of having your feet shod with the preparation of the Gospel of peace; it also has the meaning of firm footing (foundation), as in the sept. of psalm. 89:14 (R.V., "foundation"); if that is the meaning in Ephesians 6:15, the Gospel itself is to be the firm footing of the believer, his walk being worthy of it and therefore a testimony in regard to it. 1. Hetoimazo B. Verbs. (B) of human preparation for the Lord, e, g.; Matthew 3:3, Matthew 26:17,19; Luke 1:17 ("make ready"), Luke 1:76; Luke 3:4, A.V. Plan and simple be prepared means to be ready not getting ready. It means to have already been through spiritual boot camp and you are already walking in victory. It also means you are standing on God's word and you are trusting and living by faith. It means that you are prepared for the coming of the Lord and that nothing can uproot you or shake you because you are standing on a sure foundation. That foundation and rock is Jesus. And if God be for you? Who can be against you? So,stand in the liberty of Christ and don't be entangled with any yokes of any types of bondage. You want to be free and ready for his coming. Let's put on the whole armor of God and be ready for his coming.

Chapter Seven

SET YOUR HOUSE
IN ORDER

∞

WHEN YOU SET YOUR house in order you have to do an inventory of yourself and over everything that is in your house or over every one that is in your household. We have a spiritual house and a physical house. And both of them need to be straighten out. First you want to make sure you are obeying God and abiding by his laws. You want to take the beams out of your own eyes. Make sure you are living right before you try to straighten out some one else that is a part of your household. You do not want to be living one way and trying to tell them what to do or how to live when you are not abiding by the laws yourself. We are to be a holy example of God and to the world. After you examined yourself making sure you are living accordingly then we have to set our entire household in order. The bible tells us to train up a child in the way that he should go. Meaning put my words in him. Show him the right way to live. Put morals and values in him. Teach him my laws and show him how to survive so he can make it and be able to take care of himself and his family. We have to show him what God requires of him and how much God loves us all. Joshua was a example of what standing for right meant. And in Joshua 24:15 it says "And if it seem evil unto you to serve the Lord, choose you this day whom ye will serve; whether the gods which your fathers served that were on the other side of the floods, or the gods of the Amorites, in whose land ye dwell: but as for me and my house, we will serve the Lord". Joshua is letting the people know that you have a choice and an option, you can serve the other gods on the other side of the floods or you can serve the Lord. My mind is made up and I will not be persuaded because me and my house we WILL serve the Lord. I know him, he has brought me through too much. He did not give up on me and mines and I will not give up on him. He is an awesome God, and he has done too much for me. I believe Joshua is saying I know my redeemer lives and I know where my help comes from. So, if you and your family and friends want to go back to bondage and that sinful life you are welcome to do so. Oh, how we quickly forget what

God has done for us and how he kept us from dangers seen and unseen. How he gave us activity and use of all our limbs. He woke us up this morning and gave us a brand-new day. He has done so much, and we turn our backs on him. Joshua was standing on the promises of God and on faith. The New Unger's dictionary word for household"says this (the rendering generally of the same Hebrews and Greek words as rendered "house" and meaning the members of a family living in the same dwelling, including servants and dependents. So, it is saying not only do I have to teach everyone that is in my household the word of the Lord I am responsible for their welfare and care. Vine's Expository dictionary explain house as this "the eternal dwelling place of the believers; the body as the dwelling place of the soul, 2 Corinthians 5:1; similarly, the resurrection body of believers. Mark 12 :40; by metonymy; the inhabitants of a house, a household, e.g., Matthew 12:25; John 4:53; 1 Corinthians 16: 15. Now we are coming down to the end of the meaning of the house or household and describing what the responsibility is for the head of the household as far as the spiritual setting and we have concluded that he should pray and teach his family to get them back on track and in position for the coming of the Lord. We have gotten off track with a lot of things by letting things slip into our homes and allowing our family to do anything and everything in our house. So, now we must bring order back in where we allowed disorder. God is going to hold us responsible for the things that we allowed. Whatever that is broken concerning our households we must fix it. Whatever and whoever is out we need to try to help them come in. We have to present our bodies as a living sacrifice, holy and acceptable unto the Lord. It's time to get it right.

Chapter Eight

WATCH AND PRAY

IN THIS CHAPTER, I will explain both the word watch and the word pray. I will also explain the need for us to do both. When you are watching you are taking notice of something or you are observing something that is taking place. In the dictionary it says that the word "Watch" means, state of being on the lookout; close observation; to give heed to; to keep in view; to observe closely; to be vigilant; to be wakeful. While waiting for the coming of the Lord you want to do all of these things because you do not want him to come back and surprise you. The Vine's Expository dictionary describes watch as this "a spiritual alertness. When you have a spiritual alertness, your senses are overly sensitive. You are in tune with the holy spirit so you will know when things are stirring up. When you pray you are communing with God and petitioning him or making a request. Prayer is a sincere desire. It does not matter where you pray or how long you pray. The bible tells us to make our request known to God. It also tells us we should always pray and not faint. Mark 13:33 tells us to "Take ye heed, watch and pray for ye know not when the time is." When we think about the coming of the Lord most or some of us think about when he comes to rapture the church. He is coming back for that purpose. But a lot of us are leaving before that time and we do not have time to try and wonder if we are going to live until the rapture or if our time is coming sooner. Either way we must be ready. In the old testament it tells us in the scripture that there is a time to die and a time to live. In new testament scripture it tells us that the very hairs of our head are numbered. That means God has a set time for all of us that is why it is so important for us to use wisdom and watch and pray so that we will not be tempted by the devil. Jude tells us to build ourselves up on our most holy faith praying in the holy ghost. This gives us strength and builds our faith. The more faith and strength we have, the more we can stand. 1 Peter 4:7 tells us "But the end of all things is at hand: be ye therefore sober and watch unto prayer." Mark 13:35-37 KJV says.35" watch ye therefore: for ye know not when the master of the house cometh, at even, or at midnight, or at the cockcrowing, or in the morning:" 36" Lest coming suddenly he find you sleeping." 37 "And what I say unto you I say unto all, watch." The command has been given by Jesus and in the word of God more than once to watch and pray. Be diligent in your watching and praying. It is time to pray out of self. And enter into the realm of God where nothing can uproot you from his presence or his love. It is time to pray until you break through totally so when your time comes to meet the Lord your flight will be easy and your load lighter. The bible tells us that the effectual fervent prayers of the righteous availeth much. In order to avail and push through you must pray through. You must fast and pray and seek God until your prayer become fervent. Bathe yourself in prayer until your prayers get heated up. Become one with the Holy Spirit. Then you will know that you are ready and watchful for the coming of the Lord.

Chapter Nine

ENDURING UNTIL THE END

∞

ENDURING UNTIL THE END means that you are holding on until the very last end of a thing. What ever it maybe you are not giving up. In the Vine's Expository Dictionary of Old and New Testament Words it tells us that enduring means" to abide under, to bear up courageously (under suffering)". And the New Webster's Dictionary and Roget's Thesaurus says that enduring means" remaining firm under; bearing with patience; putting up with; sustaining; tolerating; v.i., continuing; lasting;" in other words no matter what you are going through for the sake of Christ you will not give up. Knowing that Christ is on his way back and that you don't want to be left behind. The bible tells us if we suffer with him, we are going to reign with him. If we go through for him and stay in him, we will have a great reward at the end of the world. And we will have some blessings even now. Galatians 6:9 tells us "And let us not be weary in well doing: for in due season we shall reap, if we faint not." So do not faint. Trust the Lord and his word. When I think about the word enduring, I think about pushing through it, fighting through it, and standing on the word of God, laying on your face in prayer, activating your faith, trusting God at his word through it all. Do not ever give up on God or his promises. Matthew 24:13 says "But he that shall endure unto the end, the same shall be saved." Timothy tells us to endure hardness as a good soldier of the Lord. Hardness do not mean that you are hard or cold in this instance, it means to be strong, be tough enough to stand firm in God, to hold on to your faith and God. To be able to take a hit or get knocked down spiritually and still stand or rise up in God. It means you are still saved, yet trusting, and yet believing that God is faithful and worthy to serve. You still have your faith and that you did not lose it. Some other scriptures tell us to be strong in the Lord. You have to be persuaded in your own heart and mind and know that God is faithful to everything that he has said and promised. Enduring means that you must be in it for the long haul. Be there until the end or until it is all over or finished. Keep living holy day by day. Do not doubt or waiver. I pray that God gives you strength to hold on and power to endure. That you will be continuing in the faith. 1 Corinthians 15:58 says" Therefore, my beloved brethren, be ye steadfast, unmovable, always abounding in the work of the Lord, forasmuch as ye know that your labour is not in vain in the Lord." God wants us and our fruits to remain until the end. He wants us to be steadfast in him so we can see him in peace and meet him in the end. So, be courageous, be vigilant, be patient, and stay in the will of God. Be in it to win it. That means run your race so you can meet God when he comes back.

Chapter Ten

HE'S COMING LIKE
A THIEF

∞

SO MANY TIMES, WE go about our daily life's working, living, taking care of the things in life to help us to survive. We are so time conscious about work and things that we strive for in life, but we are not conscious about the soon coming of our Lord and savior Jesus Christ. It is closer than we can ever know. The signs are being seen every day. Are we recognizing them or are we ignoring them? Will you be ready when the Master comes? He is coming like a thief in the night. Most of the time when the thief comes you are asleep, on vacation, at work or somewhere away from the house. He catches you off guard and you really do not know when he is coming. The bible tells us that no one knows the day or the hour that our Lord will come not even the angels know. Only God knows that great and terrible day. Do not be like the ten virgins. Because five of them were wise and five of them were foolish by not being prepared or having enough oil for there lamps. And when they left to go to the merchants to purchase more oil for their lamps the bride groom came, and they were left out. I am writing this story to open up to you about the soon return of our Lord and savior. He really is on his way back and we are asleep or in a daze or in la la land. Like the bible said we would be going about our daily business. In other words, not paying attention to the prophecies and times. The bible said that two shall be in the field one will be taken, and one will be left behind. Two will be on the house top one will be left, and one will be taken. We sometimes take the coming Of the Lord as a joke or a myth and say that they have been saying that for years. But I am here to plead with you and ask you to take this seriously. This is not a joke this is for real. Christ is coming soon. Set your house in order. Yes, it is personal, and it is an individual thing. If you look at last year along with the death of Covid-19 victims, it shows us that this is a very serious thing. That is not including deaths from car accidents, cancer, natural causes or whatever. Losing family members and friends to covid-19 to this wicked and fierce virus is an awakening to us all. My spouse and I got Covid-19 but he did not make it. And that makes this book so relevant to me. We went to get swabbed for it on the twenty-first of March, he went in the hospital on the twenty-seventh, and we lost him on the seventh of April. It went very quickly, unexpected no last words or hugs, nothing. Therefore, I believe God gave me this task to write this book about his fast approaching so that we can prepare and be ready. Not waiting around until it is too late, my husband fought a good fight, he kept his faith, and he finished his course. Now we must finish our course. He received his crown in glory. What about you? Are you ready to meet the master? We all have to cross that way one day and the bible reminds us that ever knee shall bow and that every one's tongue will confess that Jesus is Lord. We don't know when our time is up, so we have to make sure we are living all we know how to live and do all we know to do for God while we have a chance. That we must work the works of God while it is day because when the night comes, or you take your last breath you will not be able to work. You cannot do the things that God requires you to do for him when you leave this world because it would be too late. You must do it while you still have life in you. Your story is still being written for now. What will the ending say about you? Will it say you were faithful? Will it say you were Christlike or had the mind of Christ? Your father is whom you serve. Whose side are you leaning on? The song says, "I'm leaning on the Lords side." The word of God tells us that Jesus went to prepare a place for us and that he is making plans for us to be with him. We cannot do that unless we repent and serve him.

CONCLUSION

THE CONCLUSION IS THIS, God is warning us through signs wonders, preaching, teaching, evangelizing, dreams, visions, bible prophecies, and his word to show us that his Son Jesus is on his way back to claim his own. His word tells us that before destruction comes it will be a warning. We have the warning signs already. Now we need to take heed and surrender our lives unto God. Because the bible tells us that it will be a great falling away from the faith. You don't have to be in that number. God sent his Son Jesus to redeem you and I so we don't have to. The price has already been paid. Repent and be baptized. Be ready not getting ready. Remember Romans 10: 9 & 13, it's not hard. Don't let the enemy deceive you. He will never be in heaven again, but if we just repent, except Jesus as our Lord and Savior, and continue to live right you will make it in and have your crown in Glory.

REFERENCES

New Webster's Dictionary and Roget's Thesaurus Copy right ©1991,1992 Ottenheimer Publishers, Inc., 1997, Landoll, Inc. Map pages © Bartholomew, a division of Harper Collins Publishers, 1992 All Rights Reserved.

Vine's Expository Dictionary of Old and New Testament Words. Published in 1997 by Thomas Nelson, Inc., Nashville, Tennessee. Vine's Expository Dictionary of Old and New Testament Words © 1996 All Rights Reserved.

KJV Super Giant Print Reference Bible Copyright © 1996 by Holman Bible Publishers. Giant Print Concordance Copyright © 1998 by Holman Bible Publishers. Bible maps Copyright ©1998 by Holman Bible Publishers. All Rights Reserved.

The New Unger's Bible Dictionary original work Copyright © 1957, The Moody Bible Institute of

Chicago, Copyright renewed 1985 by Pearl C. Unger. Revised Editions Copyright © 1961, 1966. The Moody Bible Institute of Chicago Revised and Updated edition 1988. Additional and New material copyright © 1988, The Moody Bible Institute of Chicago.

"grammarist.com/idiom/gird-ones-loins/"

Google search/Websters Unabridged Dictionary

"ChristianAnswer.net"

The New Strong's Exhaustive Concordance of the Bible, James strong, LL.D., S.T.D Copyright © 1990 By Thomas Nelson Publishers. Appendix to the main Concordance Copyright © 1984 by Thomas Nelson Publishers. The section entitled, " Universal Subject Guide to the Bible", previously published as the "Bible Cyclopedic Index", is copyright © 1964, 1965 by Royal Publishers, Inc., Nashville,Tennessee. This revision first printed 1982.

Printed in the United States
by Baker & Taylor Publisher Services